The Sculptured Stones of Caithness

a survey

Tim Blackie and Colin Macaula[y]

With an Introduction by
Robert Gourlay

The Pinkfoot Press
Balgavies, Angus
1998

First published in Scotland in 1998 by

The Pinkfoot Press

Balgavies, Forfar, Angus DD8 2TH

ISBN 1 874012 20 2 pbk

Copyright

© Tim Blackie and Colin Macaulay 1998

Front Cover *The stone from Ballachly, Dunbeath (**8**), discovered in 1996. Photograph copyright © Paul Basu*

Back Cover *The 'Chapel Stones' site at Latheron Mains. Photograph copyright © Colin Macaulay*

Inside front cover *'Skinnet'* **Inside back cover** *'Ulbster'. Drawings copyright © Jack Saxon*

Typeset and designed at The Pinkfoot Press

Printed by Burns Harris & Findlay Ltd, Dundee

Acknowledgements

The authors wish to acknowledge the financial assistance of the following organisations without whose generosity this publication would not have been possible:

> Caithness and Sutherland Enterprise
> Caithness Council (formerly District Council)
> Caithness Educational Trust
> Caithness Field Club
> Northern Studies Centre
> Rotary Club of Wick

We also wish to thank the following persons who have been of great assistance:

> Paul Basu; George and Nan Bethune;
> Mark Dilworth; David Henry; Tom Gray;
> Don Omand; David Rosie; Jack Saxon

We wish to particularly thank George Watson of Thurso who has provided invaluable advice and support.

Illustrations

The authors gratefully acknowledge permission to reproduce the drawings and photographs of the following copyright holders:

> Paul Basu – **Front cover**
> Tom E Gray – **3**, **6**, **7**, **10**, **12**, **13a/b**, **14**, **15**, **17**, **18**, **19**, **20**, **21**, **22**, **23**, **28**
> The Trustees of the National Museums of Scotland – **4a**, **5**, **8**, **9**, **24a/b/c/d**, **25**, **26**
> Royal Commission on the Ancient and Historical Monuments of Scotland – **17b**
> Jack Saxon – **Inside front** and **back covers**
> George Watson – **27**, **29**, **30**, **31**

Country Code

The authors urge that visitors to sites follow the Country Code by closing gates, avoiding crossing cultivated fields, keeping clear of livestock, and keeping dogs under control.

Introduction

I have long been involved in one way or another with the sculptured stones of Caithness. My first encounter was being told about the stone from Crosskirk broch (**1**) when I was digging there as a student with Horace Fairhurst over twenty-five years ago. Some years later, like the present authors, I too wrote to Denmark about it without success, when, as archaeologist with Highland Regional Council, I was involved in cataloguing the stones which are now in the Thurso Heritage Museum. I noticed the difference then between what was visible on the stones in the 1980s and how they had appeared at the beginning of this century as published in *The Early Christian Monuments of Scotland* (Allen and Anderson 1903, III, 27–37) and in the Reverend Beaton's *The Early Christian Monuments of Caithness* (1913).

I well remember visiting the cross-slab in the Reay mausoleum (**12**) and being horrified to find that the work of the 18th-century vandal, who had carved the inscription 'Robert McKay 17--' in place of the knotwork at the head of the cross, had been compounded by that of a 20th-century vandal who had removed the offending inscription only a few days before. Well-meaning this may have been, but it was, nevertheless, vandalism. I also remember trudging across a wet moor with George Watson of Thurso to bring the two fragments of the Watenan stone (**6**) into the initial safety of the Caithness Museum Collection in Wick. The small cairn on which it lay had been damaged by a peat fire, and the two visible fragments were in some danger. We carried the smaller piece and, taking turns, we trundled the other across the moor on a sack-barrow. As the authors say, the rest may well lie within the cairn. I remember visiting those stones remaining outside, often in the kind of howling gale that only Caithness people really know and, in stark contrast, visiting the display at the National Museum of Antiquities in Queen Street, Edinburgh, in an atmosphere of genteel tranquillity. I recall, too, visiting the stones at Sandside House (**2** and **19**) with Tim, and hearing of a plan to try to locate another possible stone, by crawling through a stone drain where a slab reputedly had been used as a lintel. Such enthusiasm and dedication are rare!

The importance of the stones cannot be overstated. They are not only archaeological monuments, and evidence of a rich period in Caithness' past, but also works of art in their own right. The erosion and damage which has occurred over the centuries, particularly in the 20th century, is clear and unequivocal – especially to the stones which remain outside. While I for one would be loathe to see them removed from the settings outdoors where they were clearly meant to be, something needs to be done to preserve these fine monuments for future generations. A study is presently under way which is looking into just this problem nationwide. Perhaps replicas can be made before the detail disappears – although this is a difficult and costly process, not without its dangers; perhaps they should all be taken inside for protection; perhaps they should be left to deteriorate quietly and inexorably as they have done for hundreds of years. I am uncertain of the best procedure, but I think the latter course would be inexcusable. For many reasons, therefore, Tim Blackie and Colin Macaulay's fascinating survey is timely. It provides an up-to-date corpus for the end of the 20th century, adding much that is new to the works of Allen and Anderson and Beaton. The suggestions that more stones exist, previously known and now lost, are tantalising in the extreme, and I hope the authors continue their quest. The book should be on the shelves of any student of the Picts; of anyone interested in the spread of Christianity in Scotland; of anyone with an interest in Caithness; indeed, anyone with a grain of inquisitiveness about Scotland's past. It will, I am sure, be enjoyed for many years until the stones are safe or the need arises for another revision and updating of the evidence.

Inverness   Robert Gourlay

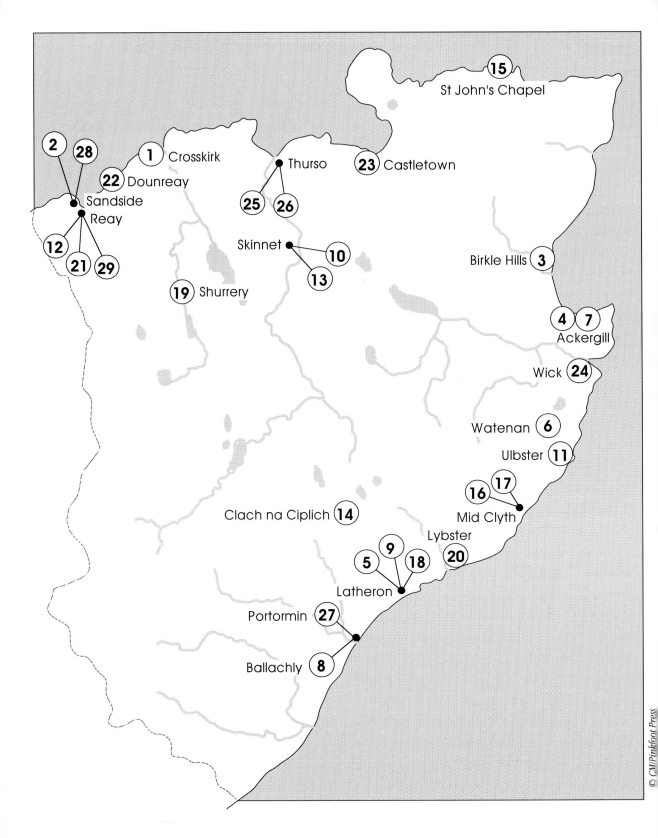

Figure 1 *Distribution map of the sculptured stones of Caithness*

Contents

The Sculptured Stones of Caithness

The aim of this survey is to produce an up-to-date and comprehensive list of the Pictish and Early Christian sculptured stones which have been found in the county of Caithness, and to provide some details about them which may be of interest to the general reader. More detailed notes can be found in the various sources given for each stone, and which are listed on page 24.

The early sculpture of Scotland has been divided into the following categories: Class I – undressed slabs or boulders with incised Pictish symbols only; Class II – dressed and shaped slabs carved in low relief, usually on both sides, bearing the symbols but also with a cross, and often other iconography; Class III – monuments without Pictish symbols, but typically having a cross in relief on one face and relief carvings of other kinds on the reverse; Class IV – stones bearing a simple cross or crosses. This survey also includes an unusual carved pillar.

As regards the meaning and significance of the enigmatic Pictish symbols, it is not proposed here to add to the already considerable literature which exists on this topic. Many of the theories which have been advanced appear to have some merit, but all involve a good deal of speculation. It is interesting to note, however, that the recent discoveries of symbol stones associated with contemporary burials in the north of Scotland have added weight to the argument that these stones were erected as grave markers or memorials.

A Class I stone was found at the Dairy Park, Dunrobin, Sutherland, on the grave of a woman, whose remains were dated to the Pictish period (PSAS 110, 328–45). The Class I stones from Ackergill (**4** and **7**) both seem associated with burials of apparently Pictish date, and the stone from Watenan (**6**) may mark another grave.

Tim Blackie
Colin Macaulay

1 – Crosskirk

Class I: 69 x 66 cm (thickness unknown)
From (?)Crosskirk Broch, ND 025 701, now lost
Stuart, I, 11; ECMS III, 30; RCAHMS, no 405; Beaton,
12; Fairhurst, 100–01; Mack, 141

Figure 2 *Romilly Allen's drawing of the Crosskirk stone*
replica (ECMS III, 30, fig 27) copied from the lithograph in
John Stuart's Sculptured Stones of Scotland *(I, pl 30)*

This stone was recorded during the last century as
having been found in Crosskirk broch near the old
chapel at St Mary's, Lybster (Stuart I, 11). Although it
was supposed to have been gifted to the King of
Denmark, there is written confirmation from both
the Nationalmuseet in Copenhagen and the Queen
of Denmark's Lord Chamberlain that the stone cannot
be found there. The nature of the stone's carving is
known from a facsimile carved in Caithness stone,
copied from the original whilst it was at Thurso
Castle. There are two incised symbols, a 'crescent and
V-rod' and an 'arch'. The former is the most common
of the Pictish symbols, and features on five known
stones from Caithness. It seems doubtful that this
stone will ever be located, but at least the facsimile
has preserved the form of the sculpture. Unfortunately,
the facsimile is now also lost although the late Lord
Thurso recalled that it may be at one of his estate
lodges in Caithness.

The latest information about the stone comes from
David Henry who has provided this summary of his
recent research:

'The stone was discovered in 1846 by the celebrated
Danish archaeologist, Jens Worsaae, during a brief stay
at Thurso Castle; it was then presented to him 'for
the museum [Museum of Northern Antiquities]' by
Sir George Sinclair, who arranged to have the stone
sent to Denmark via the Danish Consul at Leith. The
stone was found 'in a cairn (*steenhoi*)' and Worsaae
described it as 'large' but 'not very heavy'. This
suggests that it was a bigger slab than the replica,
for which, according to Jastrzebski's lithograph of it
(Stuart, I, pl 30), it would appear that a regular dressed
stone was used for copying the symbols alone, with
no attempt made to replicate the form of the original
stone. While there is no record of the original at the
Nationalmuseet, there is still the possibility that
it could be in storage outside Copenhagen, but, for the
time being, there is no access to the collections from
Esrum Abbey pending the restoration of that building'.

2 – Sandside 1

Class I: 142 x 89 x 10 cm
From Sandside Links, NC 960 652, now at Sandside
House (private)
ECMS III, 29–30; RCAHMS, no 40; Beaton, 11; Mack, 129

This handsome stone was discovered in the middle of
the 19th century on the links of the west side of Sandside
Bay, a locality which bears many traces of ancient
settlement. The stone was first used to cover a mill-lade
near to Sandside House before being moved to the house
in 1889. At present, it is placed upside-down against a wall
at the east side of the house. Two other stones (**19** and
28) are located at the west side of the house. It should
be noted that this is a private residence and that
permission to view the stones should be obtained
from the Sandside Estate Office (tel 01847 811320).
The stone is of local sandstone and is incised on one side
with boldly executed symbols. There is a 'triple-disc'

above a 'mirror-case' with a 'mirror-and-comb' below.

Pictish symbols seem normally to occur in multiples of two with the 'mirror-and-comb' often appearing in addition to a pair. The 'triple-oval' may well have had some special local significance; of the five known examples, three were found in Caithness (see also **3** and **10**). The other two were discovered at Wester Balblair, near Beauly, and at Glamis in Angus.

It is said that a former estate worker once remarked that he knew the whereabouts of up to seven other sculptured stones on Sandside estate, but he apparently emigrated to Canada and alas the information seems to have gone to the grave with him.

© Tom E Gray

3 – Birkle Hills

Class I: 97 x 53 x 8 cm
From Birkle Hills, ND 339 583, now at National Museums of Scotland (NMS) (IB188)
PSAS 29, 272; ECMS III, 27–8; RCAHMS, no 577; Beaton, 7; Mack, 35 (Keiss)

Found in the 1860s in the remains of a dry-built rectangular building during the excavation of a sandy hillock on Keiss Links by Sir Tress Barry, this stone apparently had been re-used as a paving slab. There are two incised symbols; the locally prominent 'triple-oval' and a second which has not been confidently identified, but which could be a 'triple-disc'. The stone has been broken through the middle and a triangular area in the incised face has fragmented into many small pieces. It was taken to the National Museum of Antiquities in Edinburgh where the fragments were united and bedded in cement.

Tom E Gray

© National Museums of Scotland

Figure 4a *Birkle Hills: the symbols can just be made out on the much-damaged surface of this stone*

Figure 4b *Birkle Hills: the original published illustration (PSAS 29, 274, fig 1 reduced)*

Figure 3 left *Sandside 1: fixed upside-down to the east wall of Sandside House*

4 – Ackergill 1

Class I with Ogham: 122 (max) x 69 (max) x 8 cm (max)
From Ackergill Links, ND 348 550, now at NMS (IB168)
PSAS 31, 296; ECMS III, 28; RCAHMS, no 587; Beaton, 8;
Batey, WIC 119; Mack, 29

Figure 5 *Ackergill 1*

The local antiquarian, John Nicolson, found this portion of a Pictish symbol stone in 1896, on the links towards the south side of Keiss Bay. The stone, apparently, had been standing upright within the northern end of a mound which was later excavated and found to contain another symbol stone fragment (**7**). Incised on one side of the surviving portion of this stone is the 'rectangle' symbol and the lower part of a 'salmon'. The chief interest in this stone is the incised ogham inscription it bears. This form of script appears to have originated in Ireland, and may have been introduced to the northern Picts by Irish missionaries. The ogham alphabet as used by the Picts is as follows:

B	L	V	S	N	H	D	T	C	Q

M	G	Ng	Z	R	A	O	U	E	I

Reading the Ackergill ogham from the bottom to the top in the usual way, the reading would thus be:

N E H T E T R I

Since the language or languages spoken in the area are not known, the oghams are largely unintelligible, and tend to add to the air of mystery that seems to surround the Picts rather than throw new light upon them. Whilst the last two letters of this reading might well correspond to the common Indo-European root for 'king', and the first six letters are reminiscent of the Pictish royal name 'Nechtan', this can only be conjecture at best. In any case, the ogham is probably incomplete, the top part of the stone being missing. This stone is in the collection of the National Museums of Scotland in Edinburgh.

5 – Latheron 2

Class I: c30 x 70 cm (exposed area)
Possibly from the 'Chapel Stones', ND 199 329, now at
Latheron Mains (private)
PSAS 92, 40; Batey, LAT 254; Mack, 128

Figure 6 *Latheron 2: a decorated crescent with part of a V-rod is just visible below layers of whitewash*

This stone is built into the gable end of Latheron Mains farm, which intending visitors should note is a private residence and permission to view the stone should be sought at the farmhouse. The design of a 'crescent and V-rod' can be made out (with difficulty) incised upon what is probably a fragment of a larger Class I stone, which is at some height on the whitewashed wall. The present owner has no knowledge of the stone's provenance. It is interesting to note that this farmhouse occupies the site of Latheron Castle. In the garden walling of this house is a fragment of a cross-slab (**18**).

6 – Watenan

Class I: 98 (max) x 98 (max) x 61 cm (max)
From Watenan, ND 312 408, now at Norselands
Viking Centre, Auckengill
HRC leaflet; Mack, 128

© Tom E Gray

Figure 7 *Watenan: the two fragments lie on the floor up against a wall making it very awkward to photograph them*

This stone comprises two fragments of a larger Class I stone which were found in the summer of 1977 on top of a small cairn in rough moorland near Groat's Loch, Watenan. The carving represents part of a 'crescent and V-rod' symbol. This site bears strong parallels with other Pictish period burials, and excavation could well reveal other parts of the stone.

© National Museums of Scotland

7 – Ackergill 2

Class I: 32 x 42 x 4 cm
From Ackergill Links, ND 348 550, now at NMS
(IB206)
PSAS 60, 179; Mack, 29

This fragment of a Pictish symbol stone was found during the 1920s in the course of excavations on a burial site very close to the place where Ackergill 1 (**4**) was found. The stone is incised with a 'rectangle' symbol, and below this there is a short section of curved line indicating the presence of a second symbol. This is the second incidence of the 'rectangle' symbol on the site.

8 – Ballachly *(front cover)*

Class ?III: 30 x 46 x 15 cm
From Ballachly, Dunbeath, ND 157 303, presently at
Glasgow University (Department of Archaeology)
Craven, 191; Fisher (forthcoming)

This stone was discovered in September 1996 at Ballachly, Dunbeath, in a wall of an old outbuilding which Mr George Bethune was demolishing. The building was situated a hundred yards or so from Chapel Hill, long believed to be the site of an early church building. Bishop Forbes noted in 1762 that here 'had been a small monastery of old called the Chapel or Church of Peace' (Craven, 191).

The stone is a piece of local sandstone featuring an incised design on one face only. The design is incomplete, indicating that the stone may have been trimmed before re-use. The carving consists of three arms of a cross and part of the fourth arm, plus a fish between two of the arms with its head towards the centre of the cross, where the opposing arms of the cross are joined, one axis overlying the other. The arms broaden towards the extremities, where they are furnished with a second

Figure 8 left *Ackergill 2: this almost complete rectangle has an unusual U-shaped re-entrant*

incised line inside and parallel to their ends, as well as spiral-shaped finials at each corner. At least three of these spirals feature further decoration within, including two patterns that resemble the spokes of a wheel. The fish is roughly ten centimetres long and rather crudely incised. A tail with incised lines suggesting caudal rays, at least one fin and possibly a lateral line are visible.

The iconography of this stone is interesting. Crosses of this style are comparatively rare in Scotland, but representations of fish are relatively common. Here it could be intended for a Pictish symbol, as on the Ulbster stone (**11**), and, since Pictish symbols normally occur in pairs, it is possible that a second symbol was located on the missing portion of the stone; but, given the position of the fish, this seems doubtful as two symbols forming a pair are normally positioned close together.

At present the stone is in the care of the Department of Archaeology at Glasgow University, where further research and study are in progress. It is hoped that it will eventually be returned to Dunbeath Heritage Centre for public display. It is good to hear from the Dunbeath Preservation Trust that an archaeological survey of Chapel Hill will begin this year, a project that is long overdue at this important site.

9 – Latheron 1

Class II with Ogham: 91 x 43 x 10 cm
From Latheron Mains barn, ND 199 331 (see app 2, p 23), now at NMS (IB183)
RCAHMS, no 299; Beaton, 18; PSAS 74, 534; Batey, LAT 257; Mack, 37

This stone was found built into the wall of an old barn at Latheron by John Nicolson in 1903. Both the top and bottom portion are missing. The iconography is a little unusual; the two symbols appear on the same side as a rather stylised cross, and are incised, whereas the cross is carved in relief. The symbols, a somewhat parrot-like 'eagle' and a 'fish', are rather idiosyncratically drawn. Below these, also incised but damaged and difficult to discern, are two cloaked horsemen armed with spears. This stone bears an ogham inscription (see **4**). Both beginning and ending are missing, but the remaining characters read, from bottom to top, '…DUNNODNNATMAQQNETO…'. The letters MAQQ have been noted in other Pictish oghams, and given the obvious phonetic resemblance to the Irish word for 'son of…', it has been suggested that these inscriptions record personal names. The stone was presented to the National Museums of Scotland.

It is believed that the stones used to construct Latheron Mains barn and the surrounding walls originally came from the site of the 'Chapel Stones' (see app 2, 23).

Figure 9 *Latheron 1*

© Tom E Gray

Figure 10 *Skinnet 1: the principal cross-face – difficult to photograph because of the way it is displayed*

10 – Skinnet 1

Class II: 229 x 66 x 18 cm
From St Thomas's Chapel, Skinnet, by Halkirk,
ND 131 620, now at Thurso Heritage Museum
Muir, 105; Stuart, II, 41; ECMS III, 30–31; RCAHMS,
no 299; Beaton, 15; Mack, 130 (Skinnet 2)

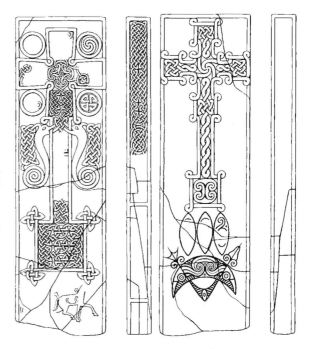

Figure 11 *Skinnet 1: Romilly Allen's detailed drawings of the four faces of the slab (ECMS III, 32, figs 29 and 29A/B/C reduced)*

This magnificent stone – 'one of the greatest wonders in all Caithness' – was excavated from the interior 'west' wall of the ruined chapel at Skinnet by the Reverend TS Muir in 1861 (Muir, 105). It appears that the stone was intact when he discovered it and had it replaced. Stuart's illustration, depicting only the front and right side of the slab (1867 II, pl 79), does not show any fracture, but misses out the bottom part suggesting that it was complete from the top to about 50 centimetres from its base, without any indication that it could have been buried up to this point. By 1890, however, when Romilly Allen saw the slab, it was lying stacked in six pieces under a bookcase in Thurso Museum (ECMS III, 31). The stone,

Figure 12 *Ulbster: reverse showing four pairs of symbols grouped round a simple equal-armed cross made up of five squares containing a continuous interlace pattern*

though badly damaged, is still an impressive monument, carved partly in relief and partly with incised lines. On the front is a cross in relief with serpentine creatures incorporated into the knotwork decoration, and below the base is a pair of stepping horses yoked together. On the back, another cross is ornamented with spiral and knotwork patterns, below which is the 'triple-oval' symbol and an elaborate 'crescent and V-rod'.

Figure 13a Ulbster: upper part of the main face showing the modern inscription

11 – Ulbster

Class II: 152 x 91 (max) x 20 cm
From St Martin's Chapel, Ulbster, ND 334 418, now at Thurso Heritage Museum
Sinclair, 139; ECMS III, 33; RCAHMS, no 445; Beaton, 15; PSAS 92, 55; CFC, 22; Mack, 131

This is another superb stone which has suffered from much rough handling over the years, but it remains impressive. On the front is an equal-armed cross with square ends and centre, above a narrow shaft and oblong base, made up of panels filled with knotwork and key pattern ornament. Above the cross to the right, is a cow. Immediately below the cross, on either side, is another animal with large paws. To the left of the shaft are two men kneeling with a cauldron between them, and below them is a serpent. To the right is a 'flower' symbol beneath which are two horses. On the reverse is a plain equal-armed cross composed of five square knotwork panels surrounded by four pairs of symbols. Beneath the symbol of the 'crescent and V-rod' is an animal with its tail curved across its back. To the left above the cross are the 'Pictish beast', or 'elephant', and 'fish' symbols. Beneath the cross, on the left, are the 'step' symbol and the 'hippocampus', whilst on the right there are the 'double-disc' and 'double-crescent' symbols. Early references indicate that this stone was unearthed in 1770 in the graveyard at St Martin's Chapel, Ulbster. Some decades later, it was moved to stand on an artificial mound in front of Thurso Castle.

Unfortunately, this stone was defaced, probably during the 19th century, with the addition of an inscription – **The Ulbster Stone** – carved in Gothic letters across the top arm of the cross.

Figure 13b left *Ulbster: the lower part of the main face. It was necessary to use different oblique lighting for both these shots in order to reveal as much as possible of the very worn sculpture*

Figure 14 *Reay 1: set into the west wall of the old church*

12 – Reay 1

Class (?)III: 193 x 102 (max) x 10 cm
Reay Graveyard, NC 969 648
ECMS III, 23; RCAHMS, no 340; Beaton, 23

Until about the turn of this century, this stone rested horizontally over an 18th-century grave in the middle of Reay's old burial ground. It was then removed to be set into the west wall of the remains of the old church, which is situated on the north side of the old burial ground.

The stone is still there but, unfortunately, behind locked iron gates, making it difficult to view. This slab of grey sandstone is sculpted in relief on one side only, but it seems extremely likely, to judge by other stones of this type, that the other side originally bore some relief work, possibly even Pictish symbols. Perhaps the sculpture on the reverse was removed when the stone was re-used as a modern gravestone. Until a few years ago, the top arm of the cross bore the inscription 'ROBERT McKAY 17[--]' (see title page), but this has now been chiselled off by a person, or persons unknown. A fine cross with short lateral arms and rounded hollows in the angles is featured, with key pattern work in the lateral arms and base. The shaft of the cross bears an elaborate knotwork panel reminiscent of the construction techniques of the illuminated manuscripts which have been dated to the later 8th and early 9th centuries AD.

13 – Skinnet 2

Class III: 150 x 84 x 13 cm
St Thomas' Chapel, Skinnet, by Halkirk, ND 132 662
RCAHMS, no 93; Beaton, 23

Figure 15 *Skinnet 2*

This stone stands upright about 1.8 metres out from the south wall of the chapel, and bears on one side the traces of an equal-armed Celtic cross, the arms convex in outline at the outer edges. The stone is very worn, and the detail is difficult to make out, but the arms were evidently decorated with knotwork patterns. A fine Class II stone (**10**) also originated from this site.

14 – Clach na Ciplich

Class IV: 122 x 61 x 92 cm
Cnoc na Crois, ND 106 395
Sinclair, 188; RCAHMS, no 149; Beaton, 26

At a very remote site on the moorlands south-west of Thulachan lies the remnant of a cross-incised sandstone slab. A photograph from the early 20th century shows

Figure 16 *Skinnet 2: Beaton's drawing (1913, fig 14) shows more of the cross than the modern photograph (fig 15, below left)*

Figure 17a below *Clach na Ciplich: the two surviving fragments* **Figure 17b** insert *this photograph, published in 1911 (RCAHMS, pl 15), shows three fragments united*

three fragments of the stone at the site (RCAHMS, no 149), but it now appears that only the two largest remain. It is, however, believed that the other is hidden nearby. This sort of monument is very difficult to date with any confidence, but it certainly predates the sixteenth-century origin that local folk traditions give (Sinclair, 188).

15 – St John's Chapel

Fragment of cross-incised slab: 86 x 58 (max) x 5 cm
From St John's Chapel, St John's Point, ND 311 751,
now at Norselands Viking Centre, Auckengill
PSAS 54, 66

In the summer of 1919, John Nicolson carried out excavations on the site of a ruined chapel about a mile east of the Castle of Mey. Inside of a doorway in the western side of the building he found a slab-lined grave, two of the slabs bearing evidence of sculpture. The stones

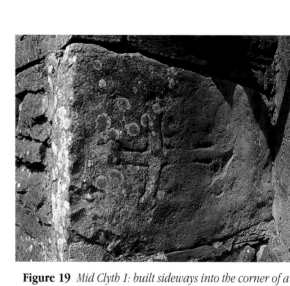

Figure 19 *Mid Clyth 1: built sideways into the corner of a wall at Roadside Farm*

were found at the end of the grave, the larger bearing a plain incised cross with semicircular hollows in the angles and tapering ends on the base and arms, all enclosed within a rectangular panel. The other slab was a fragment measuring 51 centimetres across at its widest, and showed an oblong panel bordered by two parallel lines. This latter fragment does not appear to have been preserved. The circumstances in which these finds were made suggests that the stones were re-used, but it is difficult to date them with any real confidence.

16 – Mid Clyth 1

Class IV: 104 x 58 x 13 cm
Roadside Farm, Mid Clyth, ND 294 373 (private)
RCAHMS, no 296; Beaton, 25

This stone was found a great many years ago built into a stone dyke and, having served for long after as a cover on a well, it is now built into an outside wall at the farm. Due to water running over the stone from a damaged drainpipe, it is clear that the incised cross will rapidly become unrecognizable. The cross is about 43 centimetres in length with arms some 15 centimetres long which end in round discs.

Figure 18 *St John's Chapel*

17 – Mid Clyth 2

Class IV: 198 x 53 x 15 cm
Mid Clyth Graveyard, ND 295 372
PSAS 10, 630; ECMSIII, 36; RCAHMS, no 295; Beaton, 24

At the centre of the graveyard stands this grey slab bearing on one side an incised cross of unusual design. The upper arm terminates in two spirals and the lateral arms in circular rings. This is apparently a modern graveyard, with no sign of a chapel nearby, so the stone may have been brought here from elsewhere. On the other hand, medieval references to a church at Clyth do exist.

Figure 21 *Latheron 3: built on its side into a wall of a barn*

18 – Latheron 3

Class IV fragment: 69 x 33 cm
From Latheron Mains barn, ND 199 331 (see app 2, p 23), at Latheron Mains farm (private)
RCAHMS, no 298; Beaton, 26; Batey, LAT 256

This fragment of a cross-incised slab was formerly incorporated into the west wall of the same barn in which was found a Class II stone (**9**). Apparently, a third stone which had been built into the same wall disappeared during the 1960s, so the present owner decided to preserve this one by building it into a garden wall opposite the gable end of the farmhouse that contains stone no 5. The stones used to build the barn and the substantial surrounding walls are reported to have come from the 'Chapel Stones' site (see app 2, p 23).

19 – Shurrery

Class IV: 74 x 23 x 20 cm
From Tigh a' Bheannich, Shurrery, ND 041 579, now at Sandside House (private)
RCAHMS, no 406; Beaton, 12

This slab was apparently found in a stone dyke near Shurrery, not far from what was evidently the site of a chapel; the basic features of the chapel can just about be made out at the site and large stones litter the area. The iconography of this stone is interesting. Incised on

Figure 20 *Mid Clyth 2*

one face is a small circle enclosing a simple equal-armed cross, with a stem tapering outward below. The whole effect is similar to certain stones from other areas, such as Whithorn in the south-west of Scotland, which have been ascribed to the immediate post-Roman period. Below the cross is a plain incised circle 20 centimetres in diameter. At the bottom of the stone has been inscribed the date 1911, which is when it was moved to Sandside.

20 – Lybster

Class IV: 91 x 66 x 66 cm
From Lybster Harbour, ND 242 349, now at Lybster Church
MacFarlane, 166; RCAHMS, no 297; Beaton, 25

This boulder, first noted in the early 18th century, is recorded as originally lying on a slope above Lybster Harbour at the 'Well of the Brethren'. It was initially taken to St Mary's Church, Lybster, but was subsequently moved to its current site at Lybster Church after some youths were observed attempting to roll it down the hill towards the harbour. It now lies in a rather inaccessible position, albeit protected from the weather, covered by a stone slab. The stone features an evidently natural basin-like depression which suggests that it was perhaps used as a baptismal font. The cross is incised, and consists of parallel lines forming an equal-armed cross with slightly expanded ends. The whole design measures some 51 centimetres in width.

© Tom E Gray

© Tom E Gray

Figure 23 *Lybster*

Figure 22 left *Shurrery*

Figure 24 *Reay 2:* **a** *front* **b** *right side* **c** *back* **d** *left side*

21 – Reay 2

Class ?III: 91 x 23 x 23 cm
From Reay Parish Church, NC 966 648, now at
NMS (IB267)
PSAS 84, 218

This pillar-shaped stone was found during renovations built into the south wall of Reay Church in 1947. It is sculpted on all four 'long' sides. On the front is a cross in flat relief, decorated with a diagonal key pattern. On the right side are a hound, two cows and a horse, all rather roughly executed. On the back is a stag above a knotwork panel and on the left side is a series of double spirals with the topmost apparently chiselled off.

22 – Dounreay *(figure 25 over)*

Sculptured stone fragment: Class ?II
From Dounreay, NC 980 670?, now at NMS (IB303)
PSAS 106, 230

This fragment shows a diagonal key pattern similar to other patterns found in the area. The stone was discovered in the early 1970s at the foot of cliffs at Dounreay close to Dounreay Castle.

23 – **Castletown** *(not illustrated)*

Sculptured stone (Class ?I): height 183 cm (other dimensions unknown)
From Craig of Hattel, ND 188 690, now lost
OSNB 1873 7:31; RCAHMS, no 335; Mack, 145

This stone once stood in a corner of a field near the foreshore west of Castletown on a low mound which has now been ploughed over. According to a report of 1873, the stone was sculptured with 'a very crude drawing, resembling a greyhound'. It is not known what became of the stone, and an inspection of the immediate locality has failed to shed any further light.

Figure 26 *Wick*

Figure 25 *Dounreay*

24 – **Wick**

Portable altar stone: 10 x 9 x 13 cm
From the sea off Wick Harbour, now at NMS (KG91)
Thomas, 194–5; Batey, WIC 174

For the sake of comprehensiveness, notice is given here of this small stone which was dredged up off the coast near Wick some years ago. The function of these types of stones was connected with the role of itinerant priests in the Early Christian Period.

25 – **Thurso 1** *(figure 28)*

Rune-incised cross: 84 x 15 x 4 cm
From St Peter's Church, Thurso, ND 120 686, now at Thurso Heritage Museum
ECMS III, 27; RCAHMS, no 446; Beaton, 27

This stone dates to the period of Norse domination, bearing in Runic characters the inscription 'Ingulf made this to overly his father'. It was found associated with a burial at the above church in 1896.

Figure 27 *Thurso 2*

Figure 28 *Thurso 1*

26 – Thurso 2 *(figure 27)*

Rune-incised stone: 70 x 20 x 13 cm
St Peter's Church, Thurso, ND 120 686
Caithness Courier, 30 August 1989

Built into the outer west face of the tower of St Peter's Church, Thurso, is the badly weathered remains of a rune-incised stone. It was discovered by George Watson of Thurso whilst undertaking a survey of this 12th-century church. In 1989, Dr Gustavson from Stockholm believed that the stone was inscribed for a grieving Viking for his late wife who bore the name GUNNHILDR.

27 – Portormin

Rune-incised boulder: 95 x 52 x 30 cm (approx)
From Portormin, ND 168 293, now at Dunbeath
Caithness Courier, 21 May 1997

In September 1996 four primary school pupils discovered this stone near the beach at Portormin, Dunbeath. Having previously studied the Vikings at school, they recognised the markings on it as runic script – a testament to the high quality of educational provision at Dunbeath!

The stone is an irregularly-shaped pinkish fine-grain sandstone boulder of local origin, incised with eight small

Figure 29 *Portormin*

runic characters. This inscription has been examined by philologists; early indications are that the script is unusual in a number of ways, and interpretation may prove difficult. The current weight of opinion, however, favours some sort of funerary inscription.

28 – Sandside 3

Sculptured stone fragment: 46 x 38 (max) x 8 cm
Sandside House, NC 952 652
Not previously described

This fragment has recently come to light, having lain amongst some rubble at this site for an indefinite period. The detail is obscure, and the iconography has not as yet been identified. There is a feature reminiscent of one angle and arm of a cross, which Robert Gourlay remarked could be interpreted as an 'axe shape' having possible earlier Neolithic or Early Bronze Age parallels. However, considerable doubt must remain on the stone's context.

© George Watson

Figure 30 *Sandside 3: a recent discovery*

© George Watson

Figure 31 *Reay 3: standing within Reay village*

29 – Reay 3

Free-standing cross: 129 x 58 cm; 85 cm circumference
At roadside in New Reay, NC 958 646 (? from Old Reay)
RCAHMS, no 408

This much-worn free-standing cross, now standing in Reay, is apparently without ornament. One source states that 'this is said to be the Market Cross removed from Old Reay situated nearer the sea' (RCAHMS, 110), but it is also said locally to have come originally from Crosskirk.

The cross certainly predates the Reformation, but it is difficult to date any more precisely. Such a monument would be unusual in a Pictish Christian context, and if it did indeed lack decoration, it would be even more of a rarity, but it is possible that any carving has eroded away completely.

Stones outwith the survey, and references to others

Certain interesting stones within the county do not properly fall into the scope of this survey, and evidence for the existence of others is documentary or oral, rather than artefactual.

In the graveyard at Westfield, near Thurso, may be seen two large boulders of extended oval shape, which the authors regard as natural; no obvious tool-marks can be distinguished and the surfaces are remarkably smooth, as if water-worn. It has been suggested by others that these could be grave markers of Viking-age 'hogback' type. Local tradition has it that these are the remains of two robbers, turned to stone for their misdemeanours.

In the same garden wall at Latheron where Latheron 3 (**18**) is situated, there is said to be another fragment of an incised stone, located a few inches below the other.

An Ordnance Survey Object Name Book of 1873 records that a sculptured stone was found during the removal of a broch at Sibster (ND 1499 6011) in 1841. This stone was removed 'by a gentleman residing at Thurso Castle'. No other details are known, but David Henry,

who has written about the discovery of the Crosskirk stone (**1**), has commented that

> 'the essence of this description is remarkably similar to the account of the discovery of the Crosskirk stone, and, lacking corroboration, it can probably be dismissed as a conflated report of that missing stone'

A geographical account of Caithness dating from 1724 mentions the site of a chapel 'about half a mile or less to the E. of the house of Clyth' in Latheron parish, which is, presumably, a reference to the early chapel at Clyth, of which no trace now remains. The source goes on to note at this site 'a large broad stone erected on the end with many unintelligible carvings on both sides…' (MacFarlane, 167). It is possible that the Ulbster stone (**11**) is meant here, but other accounts indicate that the latter had been lying 'on its side' at Ulbster for many generations before being taken to Thurso Castle by Sir Tollemache Sinclair. It is possible, therefore, that another such stone stood at Clyth and was removed along with the chapel itself at some date.

The 'Chapel Stones' site at Latheron: a medieval hospice?

During the course of researching this survey, the authors became aware of evidence of a previously unrecorded site near Latheron which is known locally as the 'Chapel Stones'.

The site came to the attention of the authors whilst investigating the stone Latheron 1 (**9**), which had been found built into the wall of an old barn. An enquiry with the landowner revealed a tradition that the stones used to build this barn (now in a ruinous condition) had been taken from the 'Chapel Stones', a site lower down the slope below the modern road (ND 198 328). A subsequent field visit revealed a surprising result –

a line of massive foundation stones approximately 40 metres long (see back cover).

It is the opinion of the authors that this feature can only be interpreted as the remains of a substantial stone-built ecclesiastical structure of medieval date. The site was identified as a cairn in Dr Batey's survey (1980-82, 90, LAT 258), but this interpretation must be in serious doubt. A modern boundary fence lies on the line of these stone blocks and thus gives the impression from a distance that this is a cairn of stones cleared from the fields on either side. However, the size, alignment, and regularity of the stones all argue strongly that these are dressed stones forming the lower course of a substantial building. One stone at the site, though much weathered, appears to bear evidence of carving in the form of moulded ridges, though this remains to be confirmed. An unpublished paper by a local clergyman in the 1940s gives a sketch of the site and states that it is 'thought to be the remains of an abbey' (Mowat, 26), but otherwise the authors have failed to trace any modern reference. Local traditions of an ecclesiastical site, together with the sheer scale of the structure, indicate that this was a major religious foundation.

It is possible that there is a medieval reference to the Chapel Stones site, however, as has already been noted by Dr Crawford (1982, 62) when Edward I of England sent officials to Caithness to meet the ill-fated Maid of Norway in 1290 AD, his envoys spent the night of 3 October at a place on the route north called 'hospital'. It would have meant a long and inconvenient detour inland for St Magnus' Hospice at Spital to be meant here, whereas such a foundation at Latheron would fit in perfectly with the English party's itinerary.

It is hoped that resources will ultimately be made available for archaeological investigation of the site. The wall which is visible lies on the south-west side of a roughly rectangular mound, which may overlie further foundations.

References and Abbreviations

BEATON, Rev D 1913 *The Early Christian Monuments of Caithness.* Wick, William Rae.

BATEY, C 1980–82 *Caithness Coastal Survey* (= Durham University Occasional Paper). Durham.

CRAWFORD, BE 1982 Scots and Scandinavians in mediaeval Caithness: a study of the period 1266–1375. In Baldwin, JR (ed) *Caithness: A Cultural Crossroads,* 61–74. Edinburgh, Scottish Society for Northern Studies.

CFC 1982 = *Visits to Ancient Caithness,* 2nd edn. Thurso, Caithness Field Club.

CRAVEN, Rev JB (ed) 1886 *Journals… of the Right Rev. Robert Forbes… 1762 and 1770….* London, Skeffington & Son.

ECMS = ALLEN, JR and ANDERSON, J 1903 *The Early Christian Monuments of Scotland,* 3 parts, Society of Antiquaries of Scotland. Edinburgh (repr with an Introduction by Isabel Henderson, 2 vols, Balgavies, Angus, Pinkfoot Press, 1993).

FAIRHURST, H 1984 *Excavations at Crosskirk Broch, Caithness* (= Society of Antiquaries of Scotland Monograph Series Number 3). Edinburgh.

FISHER, I (forthcoming) A cross-carved slab from Ballachly, Dunbeath.

HRC = Highland Regional Council, Archaeology 1978 *The Watenan Stone* (leaflet). Inverness.

MACFARLANE 1906–08 *MacFarlane's Geographical Collections.* Edinburgh, Scottish History Society.

MACK, A 1997 *Field Guide to the Pictish Symbol Stones.* Balgavies, Angus, Pinkfoot Press.

MOWAT, WG nd [1940s] *The Church in Latheron Parish* (unpublished typescript, Thurso Reference Library).

MUIR, TS 1885 *Ecclesiological Notes on some of the Islands of Scotland.* Edinburgh, David Douglas.

OSNB = *Ordnance Survey Object Name Book for 1873.*

PSAS = *Proceedings of the Society of Antiquaries of Scotland.* Edinburgh.

RCAHMS = Royal Commission on the Ancient and Historical Monuments and Constructions of Scotland 1911 *Third Report and Inventory of Monuments and Constructions in the County of Caithness.* London, HMSO.

SINCLAIR, T 1890 *The Gunns.* Wick, William Rae.

STUART, J 1856–67 *Sculptured Stones of Scotland,* 2 vols. Aberdeen, Spalding Club.

THOMAS, AC 1971 *Early Christian Archaeology of Northern Britain.* Oxford, Oxford University Press.